Designer: Geoff Hayes

Cover design by Julian Holland

Picture researcher: Susan Cassidy

Photo credits:
Heather Angel; Animal Photography; Ardea Photographics, Wilfrid Taylor; Australian News and Information Bureau; S. C. Bisserot; Frank Blackburn; Brazilian Embassy; British Antarctic Survey; Michael Chinery; Geographical Coloured Slides; Harewood Bird Garden; George Hyde; Geoffrey Kinns; Alfred Leutscher; National Park Service; Natural History Photographic Agency; Natural Science Photos; Ernest Neal; South African Tourist Corporation; U.S. Department of the Interior; Robert Updegraff; World Wildlife Fund; Zoological Society of London.

Macmillan Children's Books
a division of Macmillan Publishers Limited
4 Little Essex Street, London WC2R 3LF
and Basingstoke

Adapted and published in
the United States by
Silver Burdett Company,
Morristown, N.J.

1983 Printing

ISBN 0-382-06725-8
Library of Congress
Catalog Card No. 83-50388

Front cover: A rainbow bee-eater
Opposite: A red fox

The Silver Burdett Color Library

Animals

Michael Boorer

Contents

Opposite: Mare and foal, New Forest, England

3

Understanding animals

The animal kingdom is full of creatures of varied shapes, sizes and colours. Altogether, there are over a million different kinds of animals, each different from all the others. When you start to think about all these different animals it can be bewildering. To begin to understand them, you need to look for two things: you need to know what group an animal belongs to, and what way of living it is specially designed for.

Animal groups

Animals fall naturally into groups. Simply look for animals which are most like each other in the greatest number of ways. For example, insects and spiders do not fall into the same group. All insects have only six legs, while spiders always have eight.

Among the animals with backbones, there are five main groups — fish, amphibians, reptiles, birds and mammals. Each major group is made up of smaller groups. Among the mammals, for example, the groups include the pouched mammals, the rodents and the primates (monkeys, apes and man).

Sorting animals into groups is the best way to begin studying them. It helps to distinguish a whale from a fish, for example. Although a whale is a mammal, at first glance you might think it was a fish. When you look harder, however, you would notice that whales have limbs, like all other mammals, even if they are fin-like limbs. They also have warm blood and breathe air into lungs. They give birth to live young and feed them on milk, just like other mammals.

Different life styles

The kind of life an animal leads is another important aspect to look at. Every animal is specially adapted for its own particular life style. Just as a ship must be different from an aircraft, so must a fish be different from a bird. The shape, size and colour of an animal are not totally haphazard. Each feature has its own purpose.

Right: The tortoiseshell butterfly lives a very unusual life. Unlike most adult butterflies, it lives through the winter.

Insects are very small animals. Yet, as if to make up for their size, there are countless millions of them all over the world. This makes insects a very important group of animals.

They have tough armour which covers their bodies, rather like that of crabs. As well as giving them protection, it is their skeleton. The armour on the legs has joints so that the legs can bend. Insects belong to a group of animals called arthropods. This means 'the ones with jointed legs'.

Among the arthropods, insects are the only animals with the body divided into three parts, the head, the thorax (the part immediately behind the head), and the abdomen (the hind part of the body). All insects have three pairs of legs attached to the thorax. Most insects have two pairs of wings.

Insects live on land or in fresh water, but never in the sea. They breathe air through openings along the sides of their bodies, called spiracles. Their mouths and jaws can be very different. They are adapted to the food an insect eats. Butterflies, for example, eat plant matter; ladybirds, on the other hand, prey on other insects.

Above: Praying mantises live in many parts of the world, including southern Europe. A mantis lies perfectly still as it waits for its insect prey. Its front feet are clasped together, which makes it look as if it is praying. As an insect comes within reach, the mantis pounces on its victim, and eats it.

Below: This drawing shows the main parts inside an insect. Notice how the nerve centres and breathing tubes are repeated regularly all along the body. The antennae on top of the head can be used for smelling and tasting food. In flight, insects use their antennae to feel air currents.

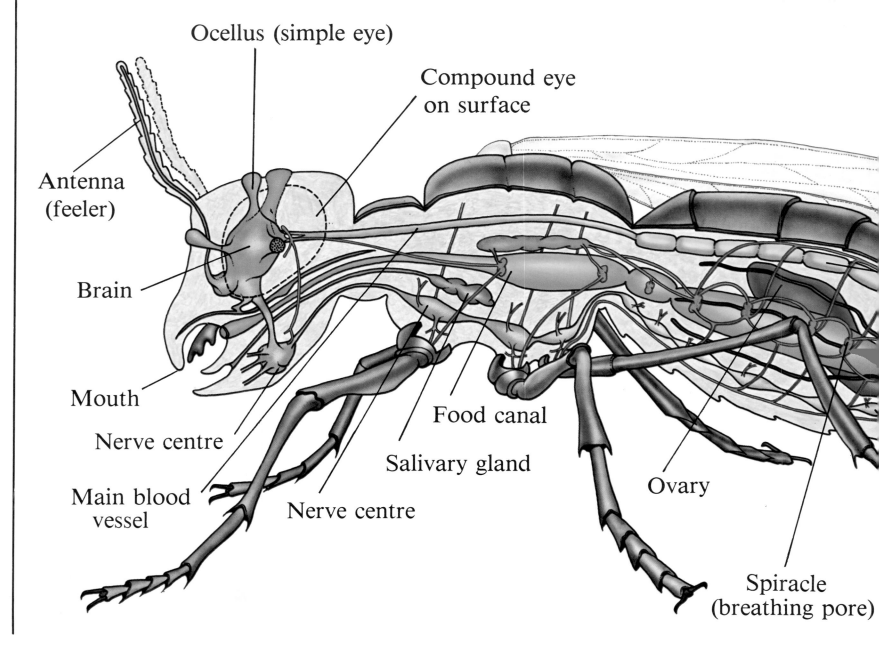

Ocellus (simple eye)

Compound eye on surface

Antenna (feeler)

Brain

Mouth

Nerve centre

Main blood vessel

Nerve centre

Food canal

Salivary gland

Ovary

Spiracle (breathing pore)

Ladybirds belong to the large group of insects we call beetles. Like most insects, beetles have two pairs of wings. However, the front pair of wings has gradually developed into a shiny, tough shield, covering the insects' backs. Beneath this shield is the second pair of wings.

Ladybirds are hunters. They feed on smaller insects, such as greenfly. They kill their prey with their two sets of very strong, curved jaws.

Dragonflies are usually found near ponds and rivers. They fly over the water hunting other flying insects. Their huge eyes can see in almost any direction.

When the dragonfly spots its prey, it gives chase. Its long wings help it to fly swiftly through the air. As it nears its prey, the dragonfly seizes it with its six legs. It holds the trapped insect up to its mouth and eats it.

Butterflies feed on the sweet nectar of flowers. They suck it up through long tubes rather like drinking-straws. These tubes are only unrolled during feeding.

Wings

Hearts

Breathing tubes

Anus

Nerve cord

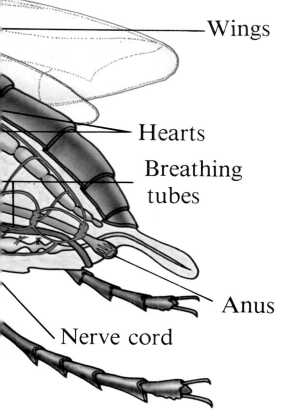

The daddy-long-legs, or crane fly, has only one pair of wings. The second pair has developed into a set of pin-like stalks. These vibrate as the insect flies, and help it to keep steady.

Many insects have these stalks, and can balance in the same way. They all belong to the large group called flies. Besides crane flies, this group includes mosquitoes, house-flies and bluebottles.

A

During their lives many insects change a great deal in shape. A change of this kind is called metamorphosis.

When adult insects mate (A), the male fertilizes the eggs inside the female. The female then lays the eggs (B). A larva (C) hatches from each egg. The larva looks very different from the adult insect. It spends most of its time feeding, and grows rapidly.

When it reaches full size, the larva seeks a sheltered place. There, its skin covering shrinks and tightens to form a protective case. It is now called a pupa (D). Inside the pupa, the insect changes into the adult. When it is ready, the adult emerges from the pupal case (E), stretches and dries its wings (F), and flies away.

These pictures show the life cycle of the privet hawk moth. In butterflies and moths the larva is called a caterpillar, and the pupa is called a chrysalis.

F

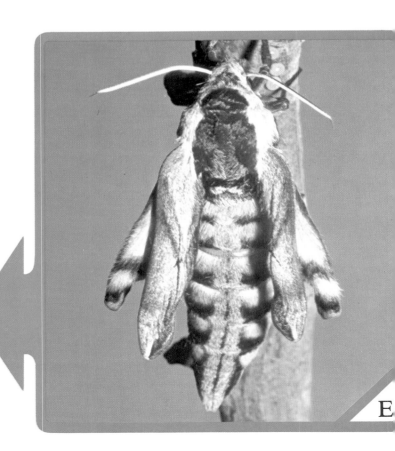

E

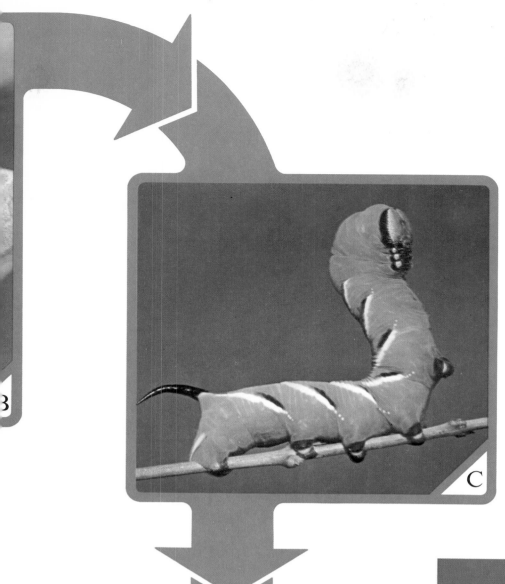

C

These emperor moth caterpillars have just chewed their way out of their egg shells. Now they will begin feeding on the leaves where the adult female moth laid the eggs. By autumn each caterpillar is fully grown. It spends the winter as a chrysalis, becoming a moth, like the one below, the following summer.

D

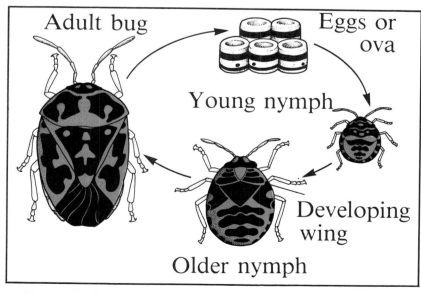

Adult bug

Eggs or ova

Young nymph

Developing wing

Older nymph

Harlequin bugs, like many other insects, do not form a pupa during their life cycle. The young insect that hatches from the egg looks very much like a smaller version of its parents, except that it has no wings. At this stage it is called a nymph. It feeds and sheds its skin as it grows into a larger nymph. In older nymphs the wings begin to show. After the last moult of all, the adult emerges. It has fully developed wings and is able to fly. The stages in the life cycle are shown above.

Male stag beetles have huge jaws which are branched like antlers. Like male deer, the beetles use these weapons when they fight each other. Stag beetles are found in oak woods.

Stick insects have thin, twig-like bodies. Some kinds have no wings at all. Others have wings which can be folded out of sight. During the day stick insects sit still on the plants on which they feed.

With their legs held close to their bodies, they look just like twigs. Even sharp-eyed insect-eating birds often fail to see them. Only at night do the stick insects move about and feed.

There are hundreds of thousands of different kinds of insect in the world. It is only possible to understand them by dividing them up into smaller groups. Even these groups can be very large.

For example, about a third of all living insects are beetles. Another large group holds the butterflies and moths with their two pairs of scaly wings. The flies have only one pair of wings. The bugs, with their beak-like jaws for feeding on plant juices, form another huge group. There are also many ants, wasps and bees.

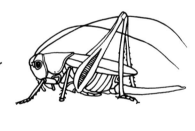

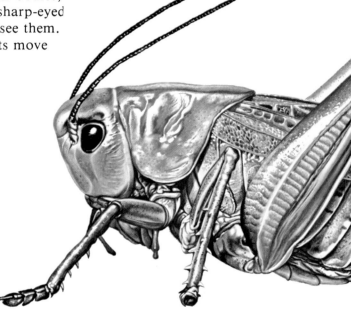

Birds are the greatest enemies of insects. To protect themselves, some insects have wonderful camouflage, or means of disguise. This lappet moth looks just like a dead leaf when it sits on the ground. It spreads its hind wings out flat, instead of folding them over the front wings as other moths do. The tiny brown scales and markings on the wings make them look like withering leaves.

Dung beetles feed on the dung of cattle and other large animals. Because they bury much more dung than they eat, they help make farmland more fertile.

Pond skaters are bugs. Their legs and feet are covered with tiny bristles that stop the water wetting them. They dart over the water surface and attack insects that fall in.

The hoverfly has an abdomen boldly marked with black and yellow stripes. Because it looks like a wasp, birds usually avoid it. However, hoverflies cannot sting. Their only defence is bluff.

Hoverflies are true flies with only one pair of wings. They hover over flowers in sunny weather and feed on nectar. Some hoverfly larvae are useful to have in the garden because they eat greenfly.

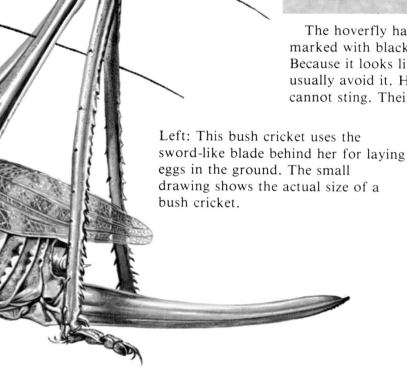

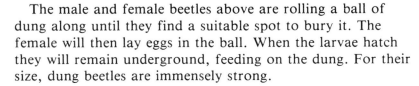

Left: This bush cricket uses the sword-like blade behind her for laying eggs in the ground. The small drawing shows the actual size of a bush cricket.

The male and female beetles above are rolling a ball of dung along until they find a suitable spot to bury it. The female will then lay eggs in the ball. When the larvae hatch they will remain underground, feeding on the dung. For their size, dung beetles are immensely strong.

Cicadas are found in places with warm and hot climates. They are bugs, and feed by sucking the sap from plants. On the lower surface of the abdomen, each male cicada has two tiny drum-like organs. On sunny days, these are rapidly shaken so that they make a shrill noise which attracts females.

Worker bees are attracted to flowers by their colour and scent. They collect both the yellow pollen and the sweet nectar, which is the food of adult bees. Some nectar is also turned into honey, which is stored in the hive. Bee larvae are fed on a mixture of honey and pollen.

Honey bees live in colonies, which human bee-keepers encourage to live in hives. A single hive may contain tens of thousands of bees. When it becomes overcrowded, many of the bees, including a queen bee, leave the hive in a swarm. The swarm settles on a branch, while some of the worker bees explore the surrounding countryside in search of a new home. Sometimes, honey bees use the hollow of a tree, just like wild bees. When they have found a new home, the bees build combs of wax, and fill them with honey. This is the food the colony will live on during the winter.

Within the hive, worker bees feed and care for the white grub-like larvae. Each larva lives in one cell of the comb. Some cells are larger than others, and contain larvae which are fed on especially rich food. These larvae will grow up to be new queens. Queen bees may live for several years.

When they are gathering their food, bees carry pollen from one flower to another at the same time. This pollinates the flowers, which can then produce fruits and seeds.

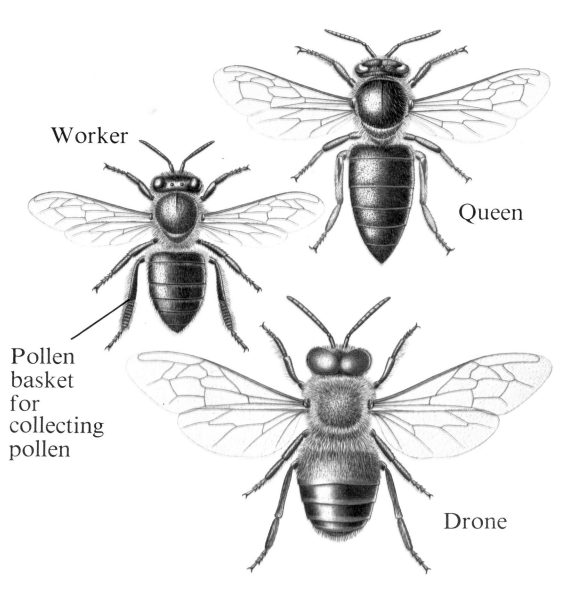

Worker

Queen

Pollen basket for collecting pollen

Drone

Honey bee colonies contain three kinds of bees. Most bees are workers, which are really females that cannot breed. They have short but busy lives. They not only collect the food, but also care for the young bees in the hive, and build new combs of wax. The young bees grow inside these wax combs, feeding on the honey stored there. The workers defend the hive against intruders with their stings. They also use their wings to fan air through the hive.

The queen bee is the only female in the hive that lays eggs. Every colony contains only one adult queen. If a new queen becomes adult, either she or the old queen must leave the hive with a swarm, and start a new colony.

Drones are male bees. They have no stings, and are most easily recognised by their large eyes. Their only job is to mate with the queen.

Drone

Drones only leave the hive to mate with young queens. Otherwise they stay at home, feeding on nectar. When winter comes they are driven out of the hive and die of cold.

Bumble-bees are never kept in hives. They are wild bees, and live in small nests containing only a few hundred workers, some drones, and one queen. Worker bumble-bees and their nests do not last through the winter. Only the queens survive, hibernating in a sheltered place. When the warm weather returns, they fly off and establish a new nest. This worker carries pollen on its hind legs.

13

Fish are only one of several kinds of animals that have backbones, but they form by far the largest group. All the 20,000 known kinds of fish live in water, although a few fish, such as lungfish, can live out of water for short periods.

Some kinds of fish live only in fresh water, and others only in the salt water of the sea. Certain kinds of fish can only survive in warm water, while others prefer cold water. The temperature of the water is especially important because fish are cold-blooded. This means that their bodies are the same temperature as the water round them. Unlike the hair on a mammal, a fish's scales do not keep heat inside its body.

Fish breathe by taking in mouthfuls of water and squirting it out through the gills on each side of the head. There are no signs of ears on the outside of a fish's body, yet fish can hear well. The large eyes, which most fishes have, can see well over short distances.

Right: The way the fins are arranged on a roach is typical of most fish. The tail fin is the main propeller. As the tail fin moves from side to side, water is forced backwards and the fish is driven forwards. The dorsal fin on the back and the anal fin near the tail prevent the fish from wobbling as it swims. There are two other pairs of fins—the pectoral and the pelvic fins. Both these sets of fins are used mainly for steering, especially when the fish is swimming slowly.

The shape and number of fins found on freshwater fish can vary greatly. The lamprey has few fins and is not a strong swimmer. It spends most of its time clinging firmly to other fish with its sucker-like mouth.

Angel fish are found in the lakes and rivers of South America. They are not difficult to keep in aquaria as long as the water is warm. The stripes on the sides of their bodies act as camouflage, because they break up the shape of the body. At the same time the stripes also act as signals to other fish, for they become darker when the fish becomes angry. This warns other angel fish to be careful how they approach.

Salmon are one of the few kinds of fish able to live both in the sea and in fresh water. They spend most of their lives in the sea, but lay their eggs in rivers. When they are going upstream, salmon can leap right out of the water to climb small waterfalls.

Rainbow fish come from Australia. They owe their name to the beautiful colour of their scales. These scales act as signals and help to attract other fish of the same kind. The rainbow fish keep together in these shoals for protection.

Harlequin fish have dark triangles on their bodies. They live in the warm waters of south-east Asia, where they feed on tiny animals, such as water-fleas. They can be kept safely in an aquarium with other kinds of fish.

Roach

Perch

Lamprey

Stickleback

Stone loach

Above: The three-spined stickleback is common in Britain. In spring, the male constructs a nest of weeds. He then swims about, showing off his handsome red and blue markings. This attracts a female into the nest, where she lays her eggs.

The stone loach lives in fast-flowing streams. The feelers, or barbels, round its mouth help it to find food among stones at the bottom. Its flattened shape helps it to lie close to the bottom of the water, out of the strong current.

Sea Fish

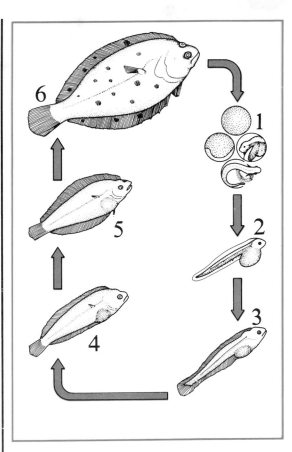

Above: The life cycle of the plaice. Eggs are laid by the female and fertilised by the male. A young plaice hatches from each egg (1). At first it is a tiny and perfectly normal-looking fish (2 and 3). At six weeks old, it is flat from side to side (4). The skull of the young plaice then starts to twist and the left eye begins to move to the right side of the body (5). It is then about eight weeks old.

The adult fish spends most of its time lying on its left side on the sea bed. Its right side changes colour to match the colour that the fish is lying on. All that gives the fish away are the movements of its gill cover and its eyes.

The sea horse lives in warm seas. It is a strange fish with no fin on its tail. It curls its tail round seaweeds to anchor itself. The female lays the eggs, but the male carries them in a pouch until they are ready to hatch.

The seas and oceans of the world cover vast areas. Different fish live in different parts of them. Some fish live in shallow coastal waters and others live far out to sea. Some fish swim freely in the water of the oceans, while others live on the ocean floor, where it is always dark.

The white shark is a fierce hunter from warm seas. Its skeleton is made of soft bone or cartilage.

The coelacanth is a rare fish that lives deep in the Indian Ocean. Cod swim freely in cooler seas, while plaice keep close to the sandy bottom. Alongside plaice, near the bottom of shallow seas, conger eels live too. Hatchet fish and angler fish live in deeper waters.

Skate are related to sharks. They have a very flat shape.

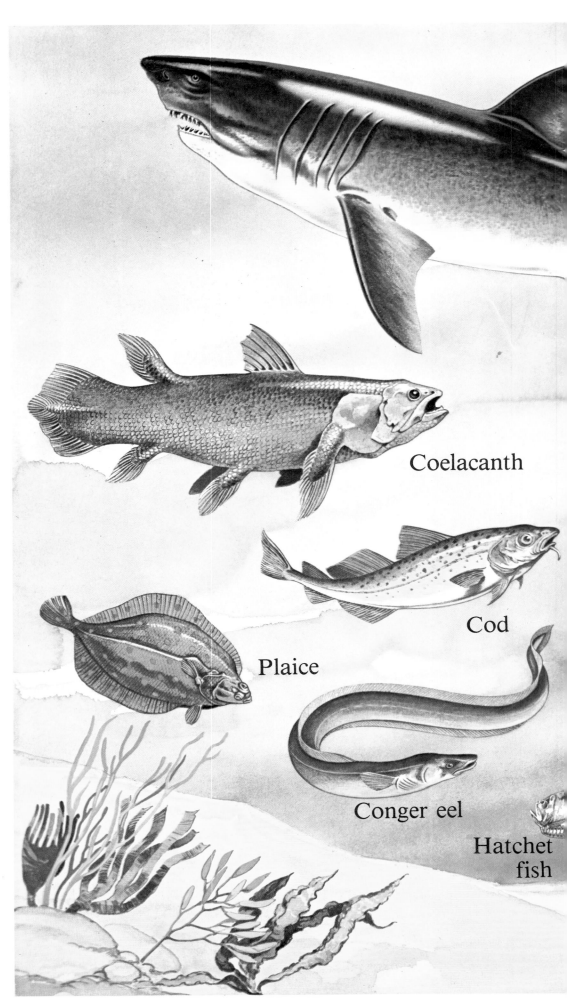

Coelacanth

Cod

Plaice

Conger eel

Hatchet fish

Below: Flying fish live in shoals in warm and tropical seas. They swim fast near to the surface, then lift the front part of their bodies clear of the water. Their huge pectoral fins then spread out like wings. This enables them to lift their tails clear of the water and glide through the air. They can stay out of the water for over ten seconds, covering hundreds of **metres in that time.**

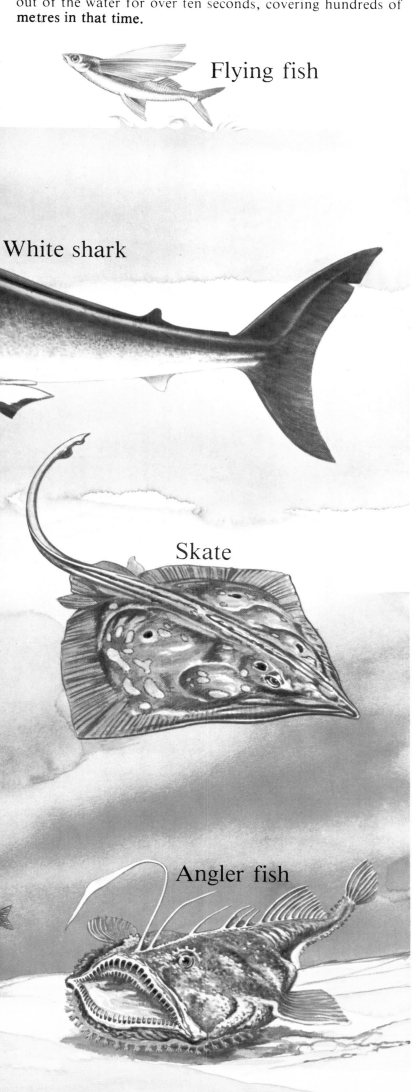

Flying fish

White shark

Skate

Angler fish

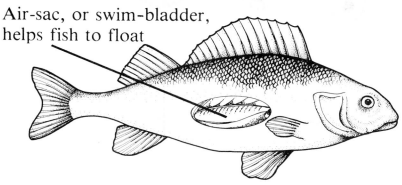

Air-sac, or swim-bladder, helps fish to float

Most fish with bony skeletons have swim-bladders inside their bodies. These bladders are filled with gas. They hold just enough gas to make fish weightless. This means that if a fish stops swimming, it does not sink.

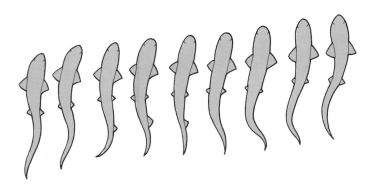

Most of a fish's body is made up of muscles. It uses these muscles to wriggle its body from side to side and from front to back. The tail lashes powerfully from side to side and drives the fish through the water.

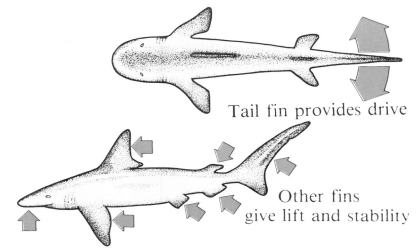

Tail fin provides drive

Other fins give lift and stability

Sharks and similar fish with skeletons of cartilage have no swim-bladders. Like aircraft, their shape helps lift them. At the front the pectoral fins work as wings, while at the back, the large upper lobe of the tail also gives lift.

Below: A flounder swims by flapping its whole body up and down. Flounders live in estuaries, usually in sandy areas.

This arrow-poison frog gets its name from the poison that South American Indians extract from its skin, and which they smear on their arrows. The bright colours warn the frog's enemies to leave it alone. Most other amphibians have dull colours which act as camouflage. Many of them can change colour to match different backgrounds.

LIFE CYCLE OF THE COMMON FROG

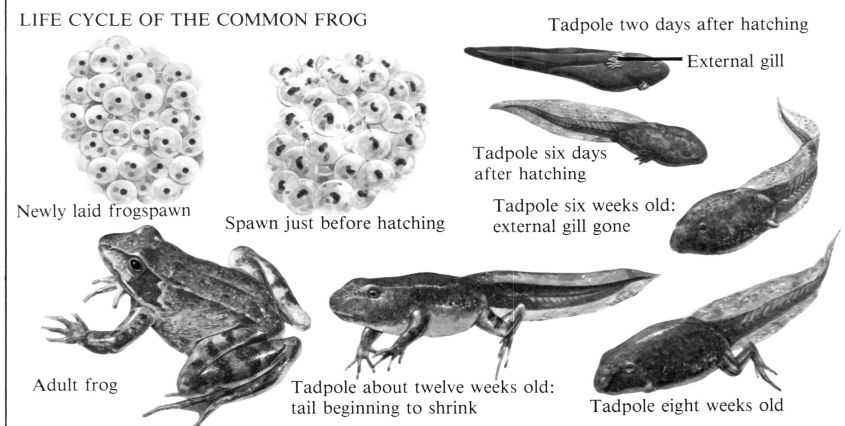

Tadpole two days after hatching

External gill

Newly laid frogspawn

Spawn just before hatching

Tadpole six days after hatching

Tadpole six weeks old: external gill gone

Adult frog

Tadpole about twelve weeks old: tail beginning to shrink

Tadpole eight weeks old

Amphibians are animals with backbones that normally breed in water. Adult amphibians usually breathe air into lungs, and can live both in and out of the water. There are two main groups of amphibians: frogs and toads are in one group, newts and salamanders are in the other.

Above: In spring frogs wake from hibernation and make their way to ponds. The females lay the eggs and the males fertilise them. The young tadpoles which hatch from these eggs have external gills and a tail. Both the gills and the tail disappear before the tadpole leaves the water.

The fire salamander lives in most parts of Europe except Britain. Its black and yellow pattern is another example of warning colours. It has a very unpleasant taste.

The male midwife toad looks after the fertilised eggs. He carries them on his hind legs, and keeps them damp. Before the eggs hatch, he enters a pool and the tadpoles swim away.

The adult smooth newt is never found far from water. It lives in Europe, including Britain, and feeds on slugs and worms. Like all other British amphibians, it hibernates

(sleeps during the winter). In the spring, the male grows a wavy fin round his body and bright colours appear on his chest. These are courtship signals.

The axolotl is a Mexican salamander that never completely grows up. All through its life it keeps its external gills, which are just like those of a tadpole. It never leaves the water.

The axolotl in the picture is an albino. That means it has no dark colours on its body. The red colour of its blood shows through, making it look pink.

The African crocodile is one of the largest living reptiles, growing up to 5 metres long. It feeds on fish, and on any land animals that may happen to enter the water. Using its muscular tail as a propeller the crocodile swims rapidly, and seizes its prey in its powerful jaws. Like all other reptiles except tortoises, the crocodile has sharp, pointed teeth.

When crocodiles lie still in the water only their nostrils, eyes, and slit-like ears can be seen above the surface. They look like floating logs. Although they spend so much time in the water, like all other reptiles crocodiles breathe air into their lungs. They also lay their eggs out of the water. Their skins are used to make shoes and handbags.

Giant tortoises live on islands in warm seas. This one lives on the Galapagos Islands in the Pacific Ocean. Some of them live for over 100 years.

Land tortoises mainly eat plants, although most of them eat some meaty food. Their heavy shells protect them from enemies, but make them slow-moving.

Above: The green turtle lives in shallow seas in most of the warmer parts of the world. It is a powerful swimmer.

Most snakes lay their eggs where they will be hatched by heat from the sun or from rotting plants. However, this diamond python guards its eggs with its body until the little snakes hatch out.

Reptiles are cold-blooded animals with backbones. They have lungs for breathing in air. Unlike amphibians their skins are covered with scales, and they always lay their eggs out of water. Most reptiles live in warm climates where they can heat up their bodies by basking in the sun.

Once, millions of years ago, the reptiles were the most important land animals on Earth. Many of them died out about 65 million years ago. Today, however, there are still nearly as many kinds of reptiles on Earth as there are mammals. They belong to four main groups. Tortoises and turtles are in some ways the most old-fashioned. Crocodiles and alligators are most like the great dinosaurs that have died out. Lizards usually have four legs and long tails. Snakes have no legs, no visible ears, and cannot blink their eyes. Some snakes have poisonous bites.

Turtles spend almost all of their time in the sea. They only come ashore to lay their eggs, burying them in sandy beaches. Because people dig up so many of the eggs and eat them, the green turtle is becoming very rare.

Chameleons are tree-climbing lizards. Most of them live in Africa. They can change colour to match their background. The top picture shows a chameleon which has just been put on a red background. The lower picture shows the same animal minutes later, turning red. Chameleons catch their insect prey by shooting out their long, sticky tongues.

The Structure of Birds

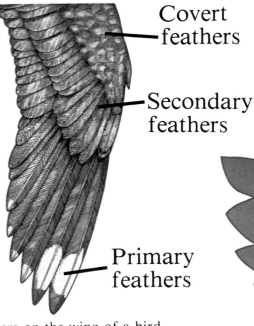

Covert feathers

Secondary feathers

Primary feathers

The feathers on the wing of a bird overlap to give a smooth outline. The long primary feathers in particular, and the secondary feathers provide the wide area needed for lifting the bird and moving it through the air.

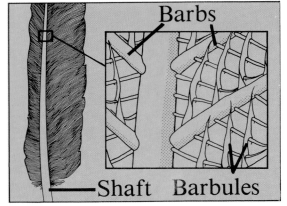

Barbs

Shaft   Barbules

Feathers have a central shaft and a vane made up of barbs. The barbs are held together by tiny hooks called barbules. Birds preen their feathers to keep the barbs in their proper places.

The woodcock eats worms and other small animals. It has eyes at the side of its head, and can see all round.

The owl is a hunter and needs to judge distance as it pursues its prey. Eyes on the front of the head help owls to do this.

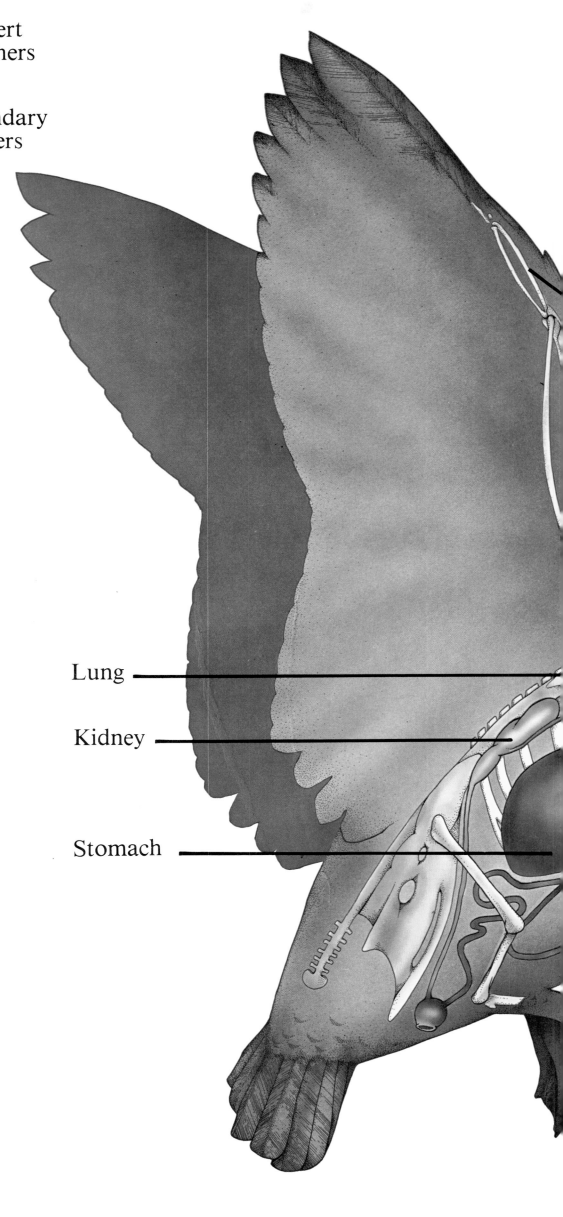

Lung

Kidney

Stomach

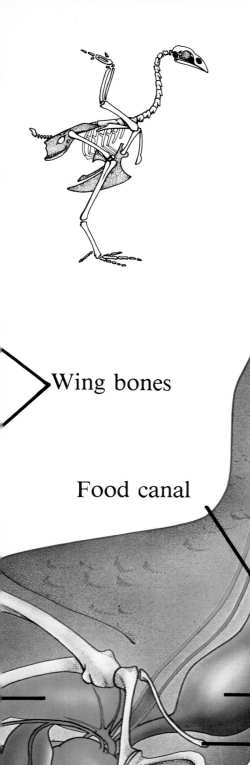

Birds have warm blood, which is rather like having built-in central heating. Because of this, they can lead very active lives in all sorts of climates. They need a lot of food to give them the energy to fly and keep themselves warm. They bite their food with their strong horny beaks. The food is then stored in the crop before it goes on to the stomach.

The picture below shows the main internal parts of a bird. A bird's skeleton (left) is light but strong.

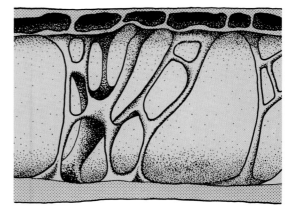

Most of a bird's bones are hollow and light. (Solid or marrow-filled bones, such as we have, would make birds too heavy to fly). Inside, a bird's bones are strengthened by criss-cross struts. The spaces inside the bones lead to air spaces inside the body. Air flows through these spaces as the bird breathes. When the bird is very active and is breathing hard, the air spaces help prevent over-heating.

Wing bones

Food canal

Crop

Wishbone

Keel

Heart

Liver

All birds hatch from eggs. Some nestlings are helpless at first. Others, like this coot, can walk as soon as they hatch.

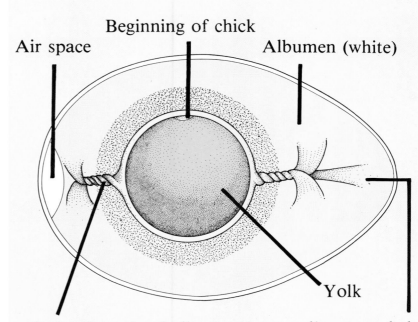

Air space

Beginning of chick

Albumen (white)

Yolk

Twisted cords of albumen keep yolk suspended

Above right: Birds' eggs are fertilised before they are laid. Either one or both of the parents sit on them to keep them warm. The young chick starts to grow on the surface of the yolk. This yolk, together with the egg white or albumen, provides food for the growing chick. Air seeps in through the porous shell so that the chick can breathe. When it is ready, the chick pecks its way out.

Flight

Nearly all birds can fly. Flight enables them to escape from enemies, to search wide areas for food and to come to rest in safe places.

The few kinds of birds which cannot fly are specially equipped for their own way of living. Ostriches are built for running, while penguins are superb swimmers.

These herring gulls are soaring over cliffs. When the wind meets the cliffs it must rise to get over them. This up-current of air provides the gulls with lift. Like gliders, they have long thin wings. Glider pilots often use the up-currents over cliffs and steep hills in exactly the same way.

Although the gannet is a large bird, it is light for its size, and streamlined in shape. As it moves along, currents of air pass over its wings. The upper surface of the wing is more curved than the lower. This means the air over the upper surface is more thinly spread. This reduces the air pressure on the upper surface, producing lift.

Above: These drawings of a pelican show how the wings are moved in flight. First, the wings move downwards and backwards, pushing the bird forwards and upwards. During

The owl is a hunter. Its large eyes help it to find food when there is very little light. Its broad wings must provide enough lift for both the owl and its prey.

Owls make little noise as they fly because the leading (front) edges of the feathers are very soft, and they deaden the sound. The prey is therefore taken by surprise.

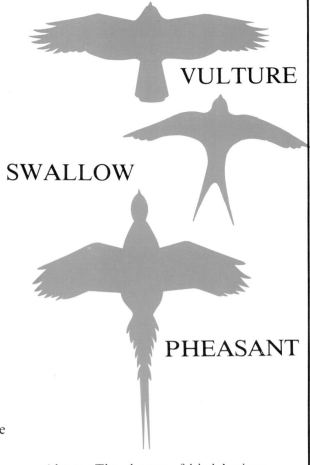

Aircraft get lift from their wings in exactly the same way as birds. Notice also how like an aircraft's fuselage (body) the gannet's body looks. The 'engines' of a bird are the large muscles which are attached to the

keel bone. The main difference between the flight of birds and aircraft is that the bird's wings must flap to give power.

Above: The shapes of birds' wings vary, depending how they fly. The large-winged vulture can soar slowly, using rising air currents to stay aloft. The swallow can fly fast and turn quickly. The pheasant can climb steeply.

the upstroke, the wing-tip feathers are parted so that the air can pass through them easily. This prevents the bird from being pushed down again.

During the upstroke too, the wings are twisted so that they move edgeways through the air and disturb it less. Like rowing a boat, bird flight is a rather jerky way of moving.

The owl in the picture is coming in to land. It flies slowly to lose height. Then, at the last moment, it turns its wings to spill the air from them completely.

Hummingbirds make a humming sound when they vibrate their wings at high speed. They feed on nectar and small insects, which they collect while hovering in front of flowers.

25

The blue and gold macaw lives in tropical parts of America. It is one of the largest members of the parrot family. It feeds on large seeds and nuts. Its curved beak is so strong that the macaw can easily shell brazil nuts.

The hawfinch lives in many parts of Europe. However, it is shy and not often seen. It uses its stout beak to crack open large seeds. It can even crack open cherry stones with little effort. It also feeds on holly berries, hips, haws, and beechmast. Like most other seed-eating birds, it feeds its young on insects.

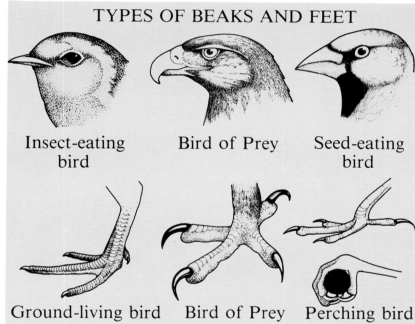

TYPES OF BEAKS AND FEET

Insect-eating bird

Bird of Prey

Seed-eating bird

Ground-living bird

Bird of Prey

Perching bird

Wrens are very small birds. They spend most of their time in thick bushes and undergrowth. They are among the most common birds in Britain. For their size they have very loud voices. They feed on insects which they pick up with their beaks.

Before the arrival of man, these hawks were the fiercest hunters to live in the Galapagos Islands. Galapagos hawks are now very rare, but they are being carefully protected so that they do not die out.

The ostrich is the world's largest living bird. It is too heavy to fly. It lives on the plains of Africa. Like the hoofed mammals, it uses its long legs in order to run away at top speed from any danger.

This male African weaver bird is building a nest by weaving blades of grass together. Once it is finished, the female will lay eggs inside.

When they have killed their prey, the hawks hold the carcass firmly with their feet. They then tear off pieces of flesh with their beaks.

Because they can fly, birds have been able to colonize almost all parts of the Earth. Only the coldest parts of the polar regions have no birds at all. Altogether there are over 8,000 different kinds of birds. Each is designed to live in its own special way. The differences between birds' life-styles show most clearly in their beaks and in their feet.

All birds, except the ostrich and the other large running birds, have four toes on their scaly hind legs. Most birds are perching birds, designed for sitting in trees. They have three toes pointing forwards, and one pointing backwards. The hindmost toe works like a thumb when they grip the branches. However, some tree-living birds, including woodpeckers, parrots and toucans, have two toes pointing forwards and two pointing backwards. Birds that live on the ground often have a very small toe at the back. Birds of prey have toes armed with strong claws or talons.

The woodpecker clings to the bark of trees with its claws. Using its beak, it hammers out a nesting place inside the tree-trunk. It probes for insects hidden in crevices with its tongue.

The toucan lives in the tropical forests of South America. Its huge beak is spongy inside and has a horny covering. It is therefore not as heavy as it looks.

Toucans use their beaks to reach fruit that is far out on slender branches. The male toucans have even bigger beaks than the females.

When a flamingo feeds it uses its tongue as a piston to pump water through its curved beak. Notches in the side of the beak strain tiny plants and animals from the water.

Like all water birds, flamingoes spend much of their time preening, working oil into the feathers to keep them waterproof. The pink colour of the feathers is caused by pink

There are always many birds both in and around water. Some eat the small animals that live in the mud and sand at the water's edge. Others, like flamingoes, sift the tiny floating plants and animals (the plankton) from the muddy water of lakes. Many kinds of birds eat water plants. Penguins and puffins on the other hand eat plenty of fish and other animals that live in the water.

Water birds have many different ways of moving through the water. Herons and flamingoes have long stilt-like legs for wading. Ducks use their webbed feet to paddle themselves along the surface of the water. Penguins use their wings as oars to push water aside when they swim.

Guillemots and many other kinds of sea birds breed in dense colonies on cliffs. Each pair of birds defends its small nesting area against its neighbours.

Penguins can move only slowly on land, but they are expert swimmers. They use their wings as oars. They cannot fly, as their wings are too small. These are king penguins.

Ducks swim on the surface of the water by paddling with one foot after the other. It is very much like walking. Some kinds of ducks dive beneath the surface to feed.

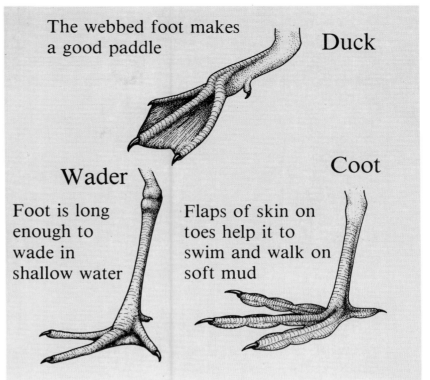

The webbed foot makes a good paddle

Duck

Wader

Foot is long enough to wade in shallow water

Coot

Flaps of skin on toes help it to swim and walk on soft mud

The feet of most birds with webbed feet, including ducks, have two pieces of webbing joining the front three toes. The hind toe is not webbed. The coot's feet are good both for swimming and walking in soft mud.

chemicals originally made by plants. These plants are eaten by the small animals which flamingoes eat in their turn. Flamingoes build nests of mud at the water's edge.

Almost all water birds have to come ashore to lay their eggs. However, the great crested grebe builds a raft-like floating nest from plants. It is not swamped if the water rises.

The puffin is not a very strong flyer, but it swims well. It dives down from the surface of the water to catch fish in its brightly coloured beak. Puffins breed in holes in cliff-tops, sometimes taking over rabbit burrows. Like the albatrosses, puffins lay only a single egg and raise one chick each year. This puffin has caught several fish in its beak.

Albatrosses spend most of their lives gliding over southern oceans far from land. They have long, thin wings. The largest kind has a wing-span of over 3 metres—the largest to be found in any living bird. Albatrosses feed on fish, squid and other sea creatures. They only come ashore to breed in colonies on lonely coasts. Only one egg is laid.

Like all other mammals, the pouched mammals, or marsupials, are warm-blooded animals with backbones. They have hair growing from their skins, and they feed their young on milk.

Pouched mammals differ from other mammals in the way that they breed. In most mammals, the young are sometimes helpless, but they always look like smaller versions of their parents. Young pouched mammals are always tiny at birth. The young of the largest kinds of kangaroos, for example, are no bigger than large insects. When they are born, they are blind and furless.

In almost all pouched mammals, the young one must make its own way to a pouch on the mother's body. There, it feeds on milk and grows. There are a few so-called pouched mammals which have no pouch at all. The young simply cling to the mother's breast.

There are some pouched mammals in South America. They all look rather rat-like, and have long tails. They are called opossums. One kind of opossum, the Virginian opossum, is also found in North America.

In Australia, there is a great variety of pouched mammals. The way they look and the way they live varies enormously. For example, kangaroos and wallabies are plant-eaters. They escape from hunters by moving fast. They live lives similar to the antelopes of Africa. Some pouched mammals climb like squirrels. Some even glide from tree to tree, as flying squirrels do in other parts of the world. There are also pouched nectar-eaters, and an ant-eater – the numbat.

In Australia and islands nearby, almost all the wild mammals were pouched until man arrived. Man brought other kinds of mammals to the continent.

The cuscus lives in the tropical forests of Australia and some nearby islands. It is a climber, and can cling with its tail like a monkey. The cuscus is active at night. It feeds on fruit, leaves, insects, small birds and their eggs.

The young wallaby with its head out of the pouch is several months old and no longer a baby.

Leadbeater's possum was believed to be extinct until it was rediscovered in 1961. It lives a life very like that of a squirrel. It climbs well, balancing with the aid of its long, bushy tail. It eats a variety of foods, including lots of insects and the nectar of flowers.

The Tasmanian wolf, or thylacine, was once the fiercest wild hunter in Australia. It looks rather like a dog, but is a true pouched mammal. It could catch and kill the largest kangaroos. When dingoes, which are true dogs, were introduced by man the Tasmanian wolf could not compete.

The koala looks a little like a bear, but it is a very different kind of animal. It is an expert climber, digging its sharp claws into the bark of trees. It is one of the world's fussiest feeders, eating nothing but the leaves of certain kinds of eucalyptus or gum trees.

The small picture shows a baby wallaby a few weeks after it is born (actual size). Already its hind legs and tail have grown. It will stay in the pouch until it is much larger.

The numbat lives in dry parts of south-west Australia. It feeds on termites and ants. It scratches under fallen logs with its claws, and picks up the insects with its sticky tongue.

The last certain sighting of the Tasmanian wolf was in Tasmania in 1930. There are rumours that it survives, but no-one can be sure. It may well be extinct.

The Tasmanian devil is a meat-eater. It was once common on the Australian mainland, but is now found only in thick forests on the island of Tasmania. It is mainly active at night when it hunts birds, snakes, and mammals up to the size of a sheep. During the day it hides in caves, or in a den among the roots of fallen trees. It is a very powerful animal for its size.

The house mouse once lived only in central Asia. It is now found everywhere. It does millions of pounds' worth of damage each year to stored food. Mice can also spread disease.

Most animals are plant-eaters. A great many small and medium-sized plant-eating mammals are gnawing mammals, or rodents. Their front teeth are chisel-shaped. These teeth grow throughout the animal's life. Wear keeps them sharp and at the correct size. The teeth at the back of a rodent's mouth grind down tough plant food before it is swallowed.

Plant-eaters are the natural food of meat-eaters. Rodents therefore need ways of defending themselves. Many of them are expert burrowers, and spend most of their time out of sight under the ground. Some rodents are good at climbing, and others are good at swimming. A porcupine's quills give it excellent protection. However, despite their defences, many rodents get killed and eaten. In order to prevent their numbers from falling, they must breed fast.

Gerbils live in very dry parts of Africa and Asia. They shelter from the heat of the sun in underground colonies. At night, they come out to feed on roots, grasses, seeds and insects. When moving, gerbils hop on their long back legs, using the tail as a rudder when they jump. Pet gerbils are usually not gerbils at all, but jirds.

The beaver is a large rodent which is good at swimming. It has thick fur which always keeps the skin dry. Its hind feet are webbed. Its broad tail is used as a rudder. The beaver uses its tail to warn other beavers of danger by slapping it on

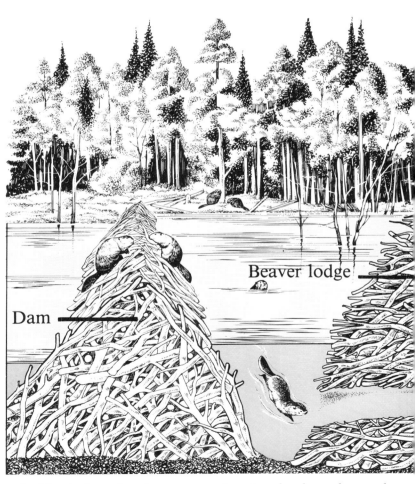

Dam

Beaver lodge

In North America, beavers use tree-trunks, branches and logs to make dams across rivers. The dam forms a pool in which the water level stays steady. The beavers build their home or lodge here. The entrances at the lodge are always under water to keep enemies out. During the summer, branches are stored in the water near the lodge as a winter

The porcupine spends the daytime in a burrow. At night, it comes out to feed on bark and roots. It sometimes gnaws at bones in order to get at the marrow inside. It moves noisily, rattling its quills, which are really long, stiff, pointed hairs. If an enemy attacks, these quills inflict deep wounds.

the surface of the water. Beavers use their front teeth to fell trees growing by the edge of the water. They feed on bark and small twigs, and use logs and branches to build their dams and lodges.

Beaver's skull

food supply. A lodge contains a pair of adult beavers and their young, which are born in the spring. Usually there are between two and four young beavers in the litter. They stay with the parents until they are about two years old.

The beaver's skull (inset) shows the chisel-shaped teeth at the front of the jaw and the grinding teeth at the back.

Squirrels climb by digging their claws into bark, using their long tails for balancing. The red squirrel is opening a hazel nut with its sharp teeth. It also eats bark and insects. In the autumn, squirrels store nuts in hollow trees and in the ground. When they are hungry during the winter they search in likely places, looking for these stores.

The red fox is found all round the world in Europe, Asia, and North America. It is adaptable, and survives in countries such as Britain where other meat-eating mammals, like the brown bear and the wolf, have become extinct.

Some foxes even live in towns, raiding dustbins for their food. In the countryside, red foxes eat birds, including poultry, and small mammals. They are most active in the early morning, the late evening, and at night.

Wolves hunt in packs. Usually there are about six wolves in a pack. Each pack is a family group, consisting of a male, female and their most recent litter of cubs. By combining their strength, a pack of wolves can kill the biggest deer.

Polar bears live where the edge of the Arctic ice reaches the sea. Their favourite food is seal meat. They have to stalk seals stealthily, because a seal can swim faster than a polar bear. Polar bears are ferocious animals.

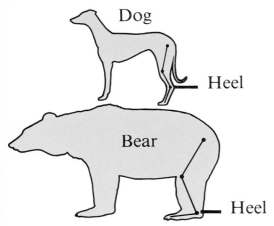

Dogs walk on their toes, with their heels well clear of the ground. This makes their legs longer, so that they travel a long way with each stride. Bears walk on the soles of their feet, spreading out their weight. They can also grip branches.

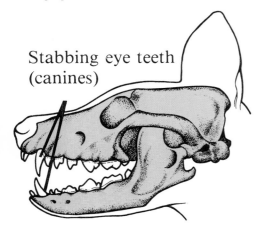

Stabbing eye teeth (canines)

This dog's skull shows the fang-like canine teeth near the front of the mouth. These teeth are used for killing prey and tearing at the meat. The back teeth cut meat into chunks for swallowing. They are also used for crunching bones, as dogs like the juicy marrow inside.

African hunting dogs live in large packs of twenty or more. They hunt and kill zebra, and large antelopes such as wildebeest.

This North American black bear is eating a deer that it has killed. Black bears are also very fond of fruit. Sometimes they use their weight to force cherry trees to the ground so that they can pick the cherries. Black bears are smaller and less dangerous than brown bears. In some national parks they beg food from tourists.

Brown bears catch salmon when the fish swim up-river at spawning time. The bears use their paws to flip the salmon out of the water.

Dogs and bears are distant cousins. Their faces in particular look alike. They both have long noses with cold, wet tips. They also have similar sets of teeth.

Both dogs and bears are specially suited to hunting. The larger, fiercer kinds of dogs live in packs. They use their keen sense of smell to find their prey. They then chase it, running swiftly on their long legs. Smaller members of the dog family, such as foxes, have to be more cunning.

Bears have great strength. Huge grizzly bears that once lived in America were able to kill bison with a single blow with their strong claws. However, bears are too clumsy to hunt well, and they often eat fruit and raid wild bees' nests in order to feed on the grubs and honey. Despite their weight they climb trees skilfully. When winter comes, bears that live in cold climates spend much of their time sleeping.

The leopard is immensely strong, and often carries its victim up into the branches of a tree. Because leopards are smaller than lions and tigers, they are better climbers. Their long tails help them balance. They eat antelopes and monkeys.

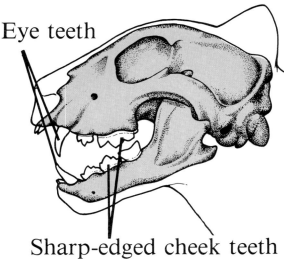

Eye teeth

Sharp-edged cheek teeth

Cats eat nothing but meat. The dagger-like eye teeth, or canine teeth, are used to kill their prey. Their cheek teeth slice meat into pieces for swallowing.

CLAW RETRACTED

CLAW EXTENDED

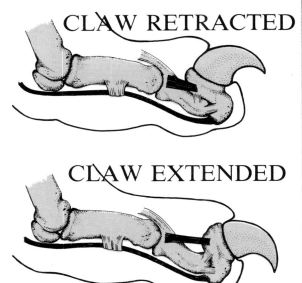

The Spanish lynx hunts hares, small deer, rodents and large birds. Hunters of this kind are regarded as enemies by farmers. Today, therefore, the Spanish lynx is a very rare animal. Lynxes are small cats with tufted ears and small tails.

For most of the time a cat's claws are retracted (drawn back). This allows the cat to move quietly without the claws scraping on the ground. When the claws are needed as weapons, or for climbing, they are extended (pushed out).

Cats are stealthy hunters. Once they have found where their prey is, they stalk it. They can move silently on the soft pads of their feet. Wild cats have coats which are camouflaged to match the kinds of places where they hunt. Using cover, they get as close to their prey as they can without being seen. When they are a short distance away they pounce, straightening their long hind legs and their muscular backs at the same time. They kill with their pointed eye teeth and their claws. Apart from lions, all other kinds of cats live and hunt on their own. Lions live in groups called prides.

The cats can be divided into three main groups. The big cats, such as the lion, tiger, leopard and jaguar can roar. They kill prey even larger than themselves. Small cats, mostly no larger than tame cats, are found in most parts of the world. They hunt much smaller prey, and have much higher-pitched voices. Small cats and big cats can live in the same parts of the world because they catch prey of different sizes, so there is food for all of them.

The cheetah is the most unusual of all cats and has no very close living relatives. It is the only member of the cat family unable to retract its claws. It hunts antelopes and gazelles in the dry, open plains of Africa and Asia.

Lions once lived in southern Europe and many parts of western Asia. Today, they are only found in one Indian forest, and in Africa. They are the only cats that live and hunt in groups. A group of lions is called a pride.

The black-footed wild cat lives in dry parts of the southern half of Africa. It is the smallest of all cats, and weighs about half as much as a domestic cat. It hunts ground-living squirrels, birds and small reptiles.

The flattened ears of the black-footed wild cat enable it to hide behind low tussocks of grass. Its large eyes can see in very dim light. Because both eyes are on the front of the head, it can judge distances very well.

The tiger is the largest and one of the strongest of all cats. Tigers live in Asia, particularly in swampy areas. They are becoming very rare.

The cheetah is the fastest animal on land over a short distance. It owes its speed to its light build, its long legs, and the powerful muscles of its hind legs and back. It can reach speeds of nearly 100 kilometres an hour. It must catch its prey quickly, for it can run at this speed for only a few hundred metres.

Walruses live in cold northern seas. The long ivory tusks which stick out of the front of their mouths are used to dig for shell-fish in the sand and mud. Walruses cannot swim very fast. On land they move clumsily.

Above: This is a Galapagos sea-lion. Unlike seals, sea-lions have small, streamlined ear flaps. On land, they can turn their hind feet forwards under the body and move at a clumsy gallop. Seals cannot do this.

Weddell seals live at the edge of the Antarctic ice. Seals swim mainly by means of their hind feet. When they are out of the water, their hind feet always point backwards, and they haul themselves along with the forelimbs.

All mammals must breathe air into their lungs, but mammals that live in the sea are also expert at holding their breath. They can stay under the water for many minutes. When they do come to the surface, they breathe very deeply, then close their nostrils and dive again.

Whales' nostrils are right on the top of their heads. The whales include the largest animals that have ever lived. Most large kinds of whales have no teeth, and feed by straining tiny animals from the sea. Smaller whales, including dolphins and porpoises, have pointed teeth.

Seals, sea-lions and walruses all climb on to land to have their babies and to rest. They have only very small tails, but their hind feet are large, with webbed toes. Seals and sea-lions are fast swimmers, and feed on fish.

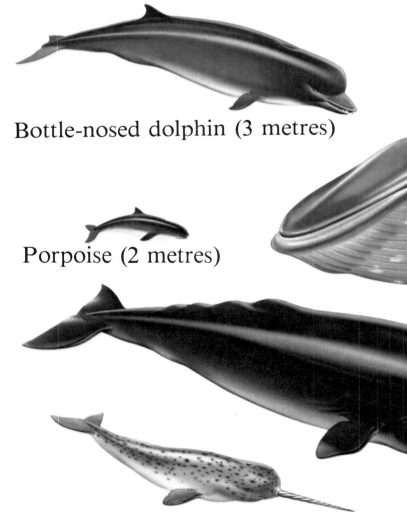

Bottle-nosed dolphin (3 metres)

Porpoise (2 metres)

Narwhal (7 metres, including tusk)

Below: Whales have a thick layer of fat or blubber just under the skin. This holds the heat inside their bodies and keeps them warm, even when they are swimming in icy seas. When a whale breathes out, a puff of vapour can be seen.

Dolphins are small whales. They are intelligent animals, and can learn to do tricks. Some scientists believe that they are just as intelligent as the great apes, such as the chimpanzee. It takes a very strong swimmer to leap right out of the water, like the dolphin in this picture. Unlike the fins of a fish, the fin on a dolphin's back has no bones inside.

DIFFERENT KINDS OF WHALES
(with average adult lengths)

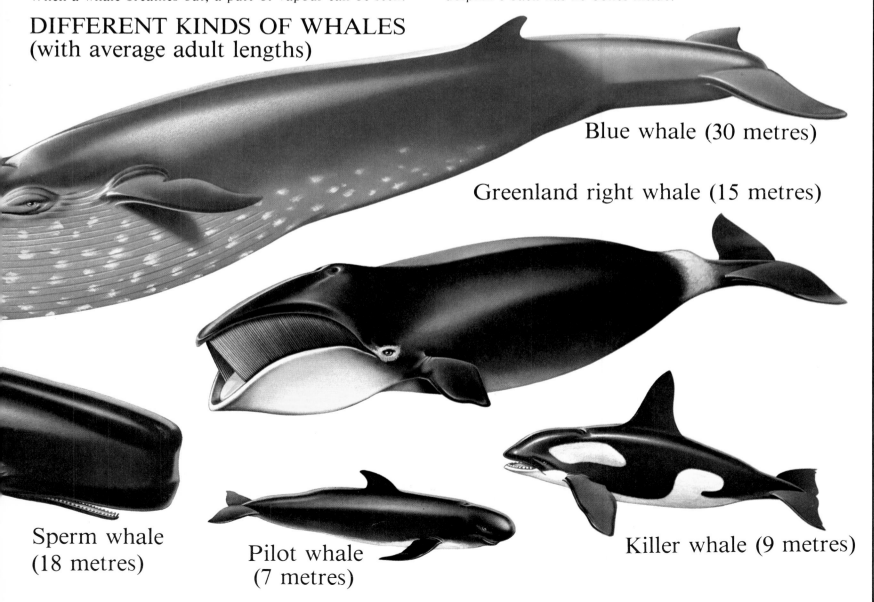

Blue whale (30 metres)

Greenland right whale (15 metres)

Sperm whale (18 metres)

Pilot whale (7 metres)

Killer whale (9 metres)

39

The white rhinoceros grazes on the plains of Africa. It weighs over two tonnes. The horns are not joined on to the skull, but grow from the skin, rather as finger-nails do. The black rhinoceros is a browser with a pointed upper lip. Black rhinoceroses can be very dangerous. They can charge at 40 kilometres an hour.

The African elephant is the largest living land mammal. A big bull elephant can weigh six tonnes. Its thick legs and cushion-like feet are designed for carrying weight, not for running.

The onager is a wild ass from Iran and neighbouring parts of Asia. It lives in small herds, grazing on dry plains. It is built for fast running. Like the related zebra and horses, it has only a single, hoofed toe on each foot.

The largest of the land mammals are plant-eaters. They need very large amounts of food because plants mostly consist of water, and most of the rest of their contents are not easily digested. Many large plant-eaters are well adapted for eating the bark, buds and leaves of bushes and trees. This method of feeding is called browsing. Other mammals eat grass, and are called grazers.

Browsers, such as elephants and tapirs, have moveable upper lips which they use to tuck leaves into their mouths. The elephant's upper lip is joined with the nose to form the trunk. Grazers have wide, firm lips, so that they can get plenty of grass with each bite.

Plant food needs to be chewed thoroughly. Plant-eaters have long heads, containing long rows of ridged cheek teeth which grind the food. They also have large bodies to hold all of the bulky food they eat.

Plant-eating mammals have two main defences against meat-eating mammals. The largest kinds, such as elephants and rhinoceroses, use their size. If they sense danger, they run towards the attacker, threatening to crush it. The slightly smaller mammals use their speed to escape from enemies.

Zebra live in large herds. They often mingle with other hoofed mammals like the gnu, at the back of this picture. The two zebra fighting are males, quarrelling over a female.

Tapirs are browsing animals from the forests of South America and south-east Asia. They have four toes on each front foot, but only three on each hind foot.

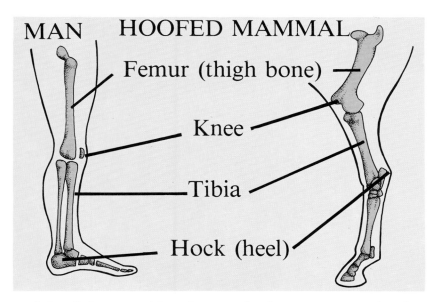

A hoofed mammal has the same leg bones as a man, but it stands on tip-toe. The hoofs are made of large, horny toe-nails. Long legs are best for running.

Female African elephants live in herds, together with their young. The bulls roam on their own for most of the time. Bulls have larger tusks than cows. The tusks are huge front (incisor) teeth. A large elephant eats up to half a tonne of food daily.

These are Russian Budiormy horses. Like all other domestic horses, they are descended from wild horses that roamed the plains of Europe and Asia thousands of years ago. European wild horses are now extinct. However, there are several places, such as Dartmoor and the New Forest in England, where tame horses run nearly wild.

In Mongolia, in central Asia, a few truly wild horses still live. They are called Przewalski's horses. They are stockily built, with rather thick legs. Their bodies are light brown in colour, while their manes, tails and legs are darker brown.

American bison once grazed the North American plains in great herds. They are now rare. About a hundred years ago, their feeding grounds were crossed by railways. Many bison were killed for food or for sport. Bison are now protected.

During the day, hippopotami spend their time in the water of lakes and slow-moving rivers, feeding on water plants. At night they leave the water to graze. After the elephants, they are the heaviest land animals, weighing up to four tonnes.

Domestic pigs are descended from the wild boar of Europe and Asia. Wild boar live in woodland and bushy country. They dig in the ground with their noses in search of roots and tubers. They are especially fond of truffles, which are a kind of fungus. Like the wild boar, the pig has large litters.

This a group of male fallow deer. Their flattened, branching antlers are almost fully grown. Soon the deer will start to fight each other, locking their antlers together and

ANTLERS   HORNS

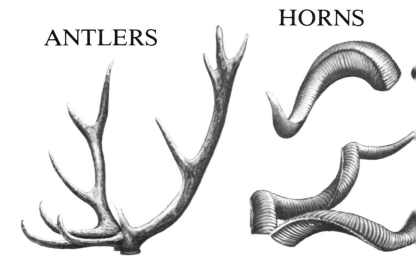

Fully grown antlers are branched. They are made of bone and are replaced each year. Almost all male deer have antlers. The horns of cattle, sheep and antelopes are permanent. They are made of horn with a bony core.

Goats are smaller than cows, and have smaller appetites. They are very hardy mammals that can eat almost any kind of plant food, including thistles. For these reasons they are kept instead of cows in many parts of the world. Wild goats are good climbers. They live up on steep hills and mountains.

pushing. The strongest males will gather herds of females, and mate with them. After the breeding season, the males' antlers drop off, and the stags form into groups again. For the rest of the year, while their new antlers grow, the stags live peacefully together. The growing antlers are covered with skin, which dies once the antler is fully grown.

Bighorn
sheep

Greater
kudu

Above right: The one-humped Arabian camel or dromedary is a domesticated animal used for riding in dry climates.

Camels can go for many days without drinking, although they cannot store water inside their bodies. These two camels are up for sale at a market.

The hoofed mammals of the world are mostly even-toed. They either have two toes on each foot, like giraffes and camels, or, more usually, four toes on each foot. In the cow and others, the two central toes are much larger than the others.

Some of the even-toed mammals, such as giraffes, deer, cattle, antelopes, sheep, and goats can chew the cud. To chew the cud, an animal first chews its plant food a few times, then swallows it down to the four-chambered stomach where the food soaks and becomes soft.

Later, the animal brings the food back into the mouth. It chews the food very thoroughly before swallowing it for the second and last time. Animals that chew the cud are able to get more goodness out of their food than other plant-eaters. They therefore need less to eat. Cows and sheep are cud-chewers but pigs are not. They are not fussy eaters and will eat waste food from restaurants.

Wild even-toed hoofed mammals are found in almost all parts of the world. Musk oxen and reindeer live in the far north, and wild camels come from the deserts of central Asia. Wild sheep and goats live in hills and mountains, and hippopotami live near lakes and rivers.

Giraffes feed on the leaves of trees. When a giraffe is standing against a tall tree, it can be difficult to see. The patterns on its body match the pattern of light and shade. A giraffe can escape danger by running away. It never seems to hurry, but it takes long strides, and can travel as fast as a racehorse.

The white-handed gibbon lives in the forests of south-east Asia. The gibbons are the most expert climbers of all apes. They spend most of their time in trees.

Gorillas live in Africa. They are the largest apes of all. An adult male weighs twice as much as a large man. Gorillas spend most of their time on the ground.

New World monkeys (from America) have flattened noses. The nostrils are widely spaced and point sideways.

Old World monkeys (from Africa and Asia) have nostrils which point forwards and downwards.

Apart from man, the larger kinds of apes are the most intelligent animals in the world. They learn to solve problems no other animal could.

Interested

Excited

Baboons are rather heavily-built monkeys found in Africa and Arabia. They have long muzzles and rather short tails. Most of their time is spent on the ground or among rocks. They live in troops of fifty or more. The leader is a strong adult male. They like to eat grubs, insects, small animals, fruits and leaves.

Like human beings, monkeys and apes pull faces to express their mood to other animals of their own kind.

This chimpanzee has been taught to undo all of the locks and bolts on the box. Some tempting food is first of all shut inside the box. The trained chimp knows that it has to undo all of the fastenings to obtain its reward.

Playful

Frightened

These pictures show that some of the faces a chimpanzee can pull might be confusing to human beings. When a chimp is frightened, it looks as if it is laughing.

Spider monkeys live in tropical American forests. They owe their name to their long, slender arms and legs. Spider monkeys eat fruit and nuts. They rarely descend to the ground.

Monkeys and apes belong to the group of animals called mammals. All monkeys and apes have long fingers and toes, with which they cling to branches. Like those of human hands their thumbs meet their fingers. This turns their hand into a very efficient kind of clamp. They are expert at climbing trees. Those monkeys and apes that climb the best are not too large and heavy.

Monkeys and apes have good eyesight. Both eyes are on the front of the head. This helps them to judge distances.

Monkeys usually walk on all four legs along the tops of the branches. They have tails which they use for balancing. Some American monkeys can even curl their tails round branches to grip them.

True apes never have tails. They never need to balance like monkeys. Instead of walking along the tops of branches, they hang underneath them by their long arms. Some kinds of ape spend a lot of their time on the ground.

Orang-utans live in the forests of Sumatra and Borneo. They feed mainly on fruit, especially the fruit of the durian tree. They live alone or in small groups. This adult male has flattened pads on the cheeks and a pouch under the throat.

Man's effect on the environment

It is no accident that most of us live in places where there are no large wild animals. Of the kinds of animals we have seen in this book, bears, wolves and beavers once lived in Britain. They have not lived there for hundreds of years, however. The reason is clear enough. There is no room for them. The people living on the island of Britain needed more and more areas of land for their farms, roads and houses. Gradually, animals like bears, wolves and beavers were simple squeezed out. Besides this, they were often hunted and killed by man. Beavers were hunted for their fur. Wolves and bears were killed because they threatened man and the domestic animals which he kept.

The benefits from man

The activities of man are not always bad for animals. We carefully look after animals that can be domesticated and that are useful to us. We grow crops which some wild animals, such as daddy-long-legs' larvae, thrive on. Vast numbers of mice live on food which has been stored by humans.

Threatened species

Civilization has usually harmed animals, however. Large wild animals most often disappear. This started to happen in China and Europe many hundreds of years ago. More recently, the large animals of other parts of Asia, Africa and the Americas have begun to disappear. In some remote parts of the world, such as the Galapagos Islands, drastic changes in the numbers of wild animals happened very suddenly.

Man has at last woken up to the danger. Perhaps it is too late for such animals as the Tasmanian wolf. We may only just succeed in saving the Galapagos hawk, the koala and the tiger. A world with no exciting wild animals would be a dull world. That is why we try to protect wild animals and allow them to survive. After all, it is their world too.

Right: Tree frogs live in trees and bushes in tropical areas. Their brilliant green colouring blends with their surroundings.

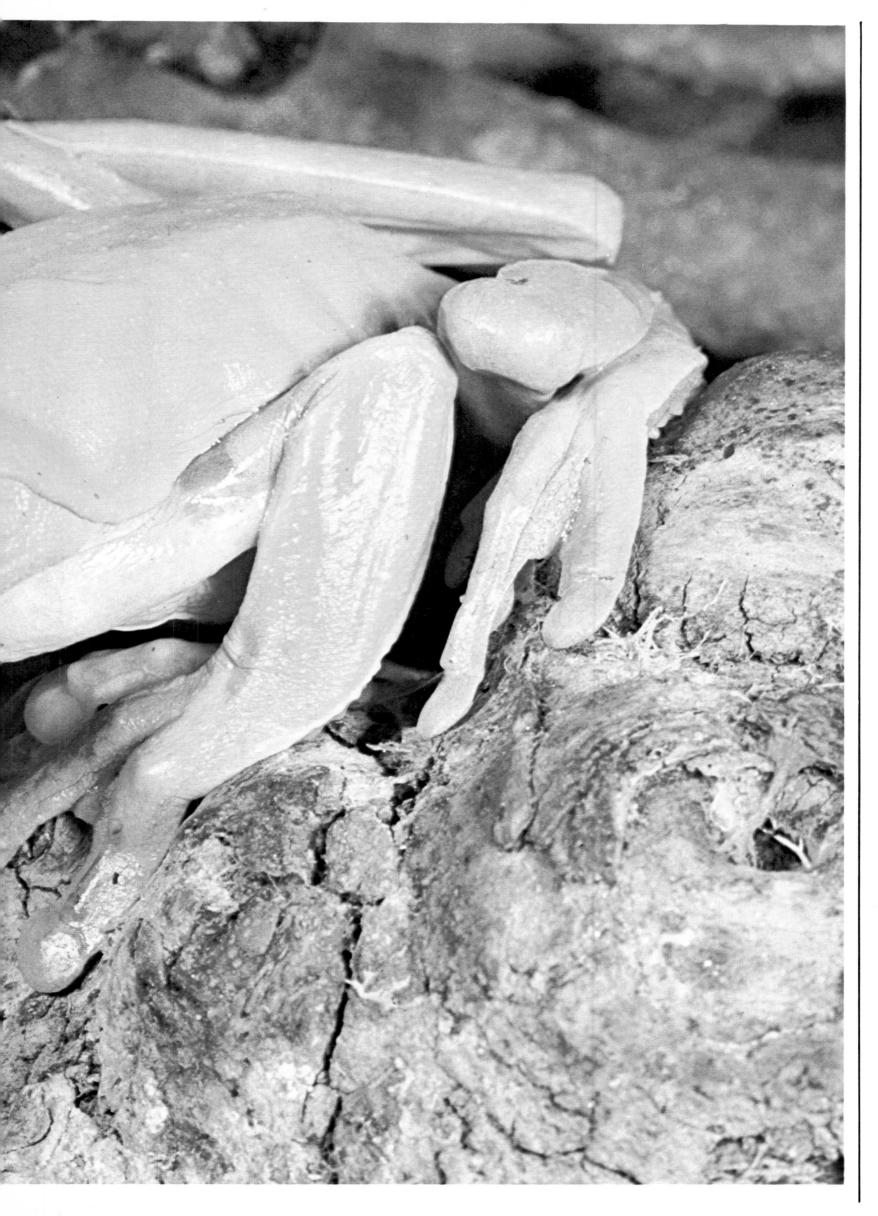

Now that you know a little about the many different kinds of animals in the world, you may well want to learn more. Looking at animals and learning to understand them is a fascinating hobby.

The kinds of animals that you are able to watch will partly be decided for you by the place where you live. It would be wonderful to have the chance to watch wild lions, elephants, and antelopes, but for most of us this must remain an impossible dream. Nowadays, most of us live in towns in countries that have become crowded with people, houses, farms, and roads. No large wild mammals can live there. In civilized countries we find mainly small mammals that are shy and difficult to study.

Because of these difficulties, many people find bird watching more rewarding. Birds are graceful, often colourful, and easy to find. Keen bird watchers need binoculars, which are expensive, but most beginners start by using their own eyes unaided. At a bird-table in your own garden or in your local park, you can easily get close enough to some birds to watch them. Most of the birds you see will be common ones. But, in a way, they are the most interesting ones. The more often you see them the better you know them.

Above: Starlings pecking at food

A magnifying glass need not cost you very much. You can use one to study invertebrates in your own garden, in town parks, and in the countryside. Look on the leaves and flowers of plants, and among dead leaves. With a bamboo cane, some wire, and an old pair of tights, you can make a simple fishing net. Such a net will have a mesh fine enough to catch the tiny animals that float in ponds and rivers. Unless you are a good swimmer, keep well away from the edge of deep rivers and canals. To take your catch home, you need corked glass tubes.

Examine your catch carefully with your magnifying glass. The best way to make quite sure that you look at it hard enough is to draw it. Use a sharp pencil and draw clear, neat lines. Your aim is to draw the outline of all the parts of the animal that you can see. You will find that your drawings improve with practice.

Once you have your drawing, the wisest thing to do is to release the animals close to the place where you found them. Only if you are quite sure you know what kind of animal you have caught, and know how to look after it, should you consider keeping it. Remember that caring for animals can take up a great deal of your time.

Above: Well-stocked bookshelf of a children's library

If you cannot identify your animals, don't be disappointed. Even in town gardens there are so many kinds of invertebrates that few, if any, adult experts could know all of their names. What you must do is to get help. There may be a teacher at your school who can tell you where to find out what you want to know. If your local museum has a natural history department, someone there can help. There may be a local natural history society that you can join, in order to learn from other people. If all this fails, go to your local library and explain your problems. Somewhere there will be a book with words and pictures which will tell you what you want to know.

Remember, to begin to understand an animal, it helps to know what group of animals it belongs to.

Each animal that you find is part of a miniature world that includes hunters and hunted animals, burrowers, runners, fliers and swimmers.

Above: Feeding-time for the sea-lions at a zoo in Stuttgart, W. Germany

If you feel that large animals are the most interesting, do not despair. You can learn something from watching tame ones. One expert on wild cats began his studies by watching the movements of tame cats from his bedroom window when he was ill. Alternatively you can visit your nearest zoo. The animals there are all members of groups, just like the animals in your own back garden.

Above: Observing animals from a special train at Whipsnade Zoo, England

Books can be a great help. However, they cannot tell you everything. The best way to learn about animals is to look at them for yourself, and watch how they behave. Then think about what you see, and try to make sense of it.